LONDON, NEW YORK, MELBOURNE, MUNICH, AND DELHI

Editor James Mitchem
Senior Designer Wendy Bartlet
Designer Poppy Joslin
Photography Dave King
Additional editing Becky Alexander, Grace Redhead
US Editor Margaret Parrish
Additional design Jess Bentall
Managing Editor Penny Smith
Managing Art Editor Marianne Markham
Art Director Jane Bull
Category Publisher Mary Ling
Production Editor Raymond Williams
Senior Production Controller Seyhan Esen
Jacket Designer Wendy Bartlet
Creative Technical Support Sonia Charbonnier

First published in the United States in 2013 by
DK Publishing, 345 Hudson Street, New York, New York 10014
Copyright© 2013 Dorling Kindersley Limited
13 14 15 16 17 10 9 8 7 6 5 4 3 2
002—185649—04/13

A catalog record for this book is available from the Library of Congress.
ISBN: 978-1-4654-0256-1
Printed and bound in China By South China Co. Ltd.

Discover more at www.dk.com

The BIG BOOK of Crafts & Activities

Contents

SAFETY

This book is packed with activities—some are simple, while others are trickier. We hope you enjoy this book, but please be sensible and safe. Only attempt anything potentially dangerous, such as cooking or cutting, under the supervision of an adult.

The authors and publisher cannot take responsibility for the outcome, injury, loss, damage, or mess that occurs as a result of you attempting the activities in this book. Tell an adult before you do any of them, read all instructions carefully, and seek help when you need it.

Make a bulletin board

You will need
- Cotton fabric
- Polyester batting
- Cork bulletin board
- Staple gun and staples
- Ribbon • Tape
- Thumbtacks

Bulletin boards are great for collecting your favorite odds and ends: photos, sketches, notes—anything you like! The best part is picking your fabric and making your bulletin board look beautiful.

The fabric needs to go at the bottom

The batting goes between the board and fabric

The board needs to be right in the center

1. In order, put the fabric, the batting, and the bulletin board down on a flat surface. Lay the bulletin board with the cork side facedown.

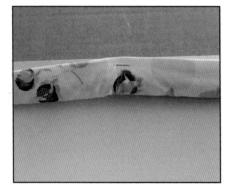

2. Fold the batting and fabric up at one side and get an adult to staple it in the middle. Do this for all four sides, making sure it's pulled tight.

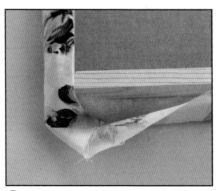

3. For the corners, tuck one side of the fabric down into the other and fold the other side up, as shown. Make sure it's nice and neat.

4. Once you've tucked in the corner neatly, get an adult to staple it in place on both sides. Do this for the other corners, too.

You can make the ribbon run like this, too

Use colored thumbtacks to match your fabric

5. Spread strips of ribbon across the front diagonally and tape them in place. Turn the board over and get an adult to staple the ribbon to it.

6. Remove the tape and lay more ribbon across to create a pattern. Tape in place each time, and get an adult to staple it to the back.

7. Push in thumbtacks where the pieces of ribbon meet to keep them in place. Now add whatever you want to feature on your bulletin board.

Try to use the fanciest frame you can find

Framed bulletin board

Now that you know how to make a basic bulletin board, get creative and add a frame. For even greater effect, choose one with lots of decoration and really make your bulletin board stand out.

You will need
- Picture frame
- Cork tile
- Emulsion paint
- Cotton fabric
- Scissors
- Staple gun or glue

If you're using a staple gun, ask an adult to help

1. Find a frame that's the right size to hold a cork tile. Paint with the emulsion paint and let dry.

2. Cut out the fabric and lay it underneath the cork tile, leaving some extra room on all sides to fold it over.

3. Fold the fabric over the back, tuck in the corners, and staple them in place. Put your board in the frame.

Pretty hangers

Pretty clothes belong on a pretty hanger. Unfortunately, most hangers are boring. Luckily for you, you can decorate these hangers so they look as good as your clothes!

You will need

- Wooden hangers
- Paper • Pencil
- Felt • Pins
- Polyester batting
- Needle and thread

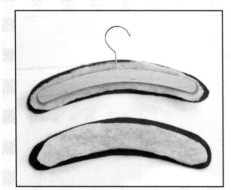

1. Lay a wooden hanger out on a piece of paper and draw around it, leaving a gap of about 1in (2.5cm) all around.

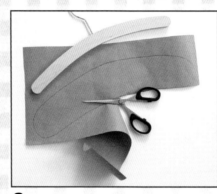

2. Carefully cut the shape out to create a template. You can use this template to decorate as many hangers as you like.

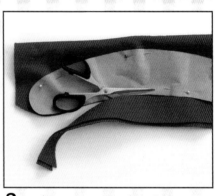

3. Fold a piece of felt in half and pin the template to it. Cut around it so that you have two identical pieces of felt. Remove the pins.

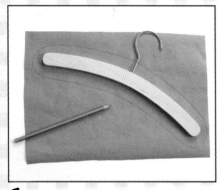

4. Cut a piece of batting that is smaller than the felt but bigger than the hanger. Lay it on top of the felt, then put the hanger on top.

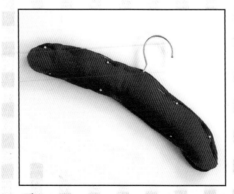

5. Put another strip of batting and the other piece of felt on top of the hanger. Insert pins along the edges to keep everything in place.

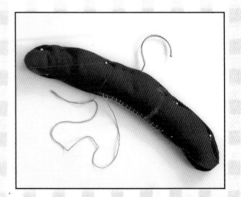

6. Use the needle and thread to stitch the felt together. Ask an adult to help you with this. Remove the pins and decorate!

Cut flowers out of felt scraps and glue or stitch them to your hanger

Furniture makeover

When you're in the process of giving your bedroom a makeover, a few posters will only go so far. If you have old furniture, you can give it a new lease on life with paint and decorations (if your parents agree!).

You will need
- Old furniture
- Sandpaper
- Primer paint
- Satin enamel paint
- Ribbons, glue, and trim
- Hair clips

1. Rub a plain old table with sandpaper to remove any rough spots. Wipe it with a cloth to get rid of dust, then paint it with a layer of primer paint.

2. Once the primer has dried, paint the table in your favorite colors using satin enamel paint and let dry. Try not to let any of the paint drip.

1. Rub the chair with sandpaper, as above, and apply a layer of primer paint. Make sure you cover the chair completely, painting behind the legs, too.

2. Paint the chair carefully with satin enamel paint. Make sure you get into all the corners so it looks neat and tidy.

Cut the ribbon so it doesn't drag on the floor

3. Wrap ribbon around the sides and pedestal of the table and glue it in place. Next, glue some trim around the edge of the table.

Use different colored ribbons for the base

3. Loop pieces of different colored ribbons over the back, and use hair clips to hold them in place.

More furniture

Now that you've mastered decorating chairs and tables, try decorating a nightstand or dresser—that will really breathe new life into your bedroom. Here's a suggestion for how to do it.

1. Unscrew the knob. Use sandpaper to sand the furniture. Paint with primer and let dry. Paint with satin paint.

2. Once the paint has dried, measure the side panel with a ruler and cut out a piece of cardboard the same size.

3. Lay the cardboard on top of your chosen fabric. Fold over the edges and either glue or staple them in place.

4. Glue the cardboard to the side of the nightstand and then repeat this for the other side and the front.

5. Cut out a circle of fabric to cover the knob. Put the knob in the middle of the fabric. Scrunch it around the knob.

6. Tie the fabric in place with narrow ribbon. Trim off excess fabric and screw the knob in place.

Choose fabric and paint that go together: this paint color matches the yellow petals in the fabric pattern

Colorful fabric
makes your
furniture unique

Use enough ribbon
so that it hangs down
and looks stylish

Perfect pillows

Adding a fabric picture to a plain old pillow is a great way to make it stand out. Here's how to make one with a strawberry motif—but you can use any shape or design you like.

You will need
- Pencil and paper
- Iron • Fusible webbing
- Fabric • Pillow cover
- Needle and thread

1. Neatly draw your strawberry on a piece of paper and place the fusible webbing on top. Trace around the strawberry and cut it out.

2. Ask an adult to iron the fusible webbing shapes onto colored fabric. Use red for the strawberry and green for the leaves.

3. Cut around the fabric and fusible webbing carefully. Try to be as neat as you can.

4. Lay your design with the fusible webbing side facedown on the pillow cover. Ask an adult to iron the shapes.

5. Use a needle and thread to sew around your strawberry to add decoration and to help keep it in place.

6. Sew green thread around the leaves and stalk. Use either white or yellow thread on the strawberry to make the seeds.

Why not decorate more pillows in other motifs? Make one raspberry and one red flower pillow and you have a set!

Pamper day

Which one is your favorite?

The next time you want to feel pampered, treat yourself and your friends to a home spa day, complete with face masks and smoothies.

Fruit smoothies are a delicious, healthy treat. To make them, all you do is purée the ingredients together in a blender. Add a few ice cubes if you like, and serve with some fresh berries on top.

Blackberry and Blueberry

Ingredients

- ½ cup blackberries
- ½ cup strawberries, quartered
- ¼ cup blueberries
- ¼ banana
- 4 tbsp blueberry yogurt
- 2 tsp honey

Face masks

Face masks are a great way to refresh your skin. All you need are a few ingredients from home, such as bananas and honey! Apply the mask to your face and rinse it off with warm water after 10 minutes.

Yogurt and egg whites

Crack two eggs and discard the yolks. Put the egg whites in a bowl and add 2 tbsp of plain yogurt (don't use flavored yogurt!) Mix together until smooth.

Banana and honey

Mash a banana with 1 tbsp honey and a drop of orange juice. Mix until smooth.

Avocado and honey

Mash an avocado and ½ cup honey in a bowl. Mix together until smooth.

Strawberry and Honey

Ingredients
- ¾ cup strawberries, quartered
- ¼ banana
- 2 tsp honey
- 6 tbsp strawberry yogurt

Tropical Banana

Ingredients
- 1 mango, chopped
- ¼ banana
- ¼ cup pineapple chunks
- 6 tbsp pineapple juice
- ¼ cup vanilla yogurt

Banana Caramel

Drizzle caramel on top!

Ingredients
- 2½ tbsp dulche de leche
- ½ cup milk
- 1 banana
- ¼ cup plain yogurt

Bath bombs

A lot of people add bubbles to their baths to make them more fun. But if you drop a bath bomb into the tub instead it will fizz and pop, adding color and a lovely smell to the bathwater. That's even better than bubbles!

You will need

- 1 cup baking soda
- ½ cup citric acid powder
- Food coloring
- 2 tbsp olive oil

- Scented oil
- Spray bottle
- Witch hazel
- Plastic molds
- Sprinkles or cake decorations

1. Pour the baking soda and citric acid into a large mixing bowl.

2. Add several drops of food coloring and stir it in well. Use whatever color you like.

3. Add the olive oil. Sprinkle it evenly over the surface of the mixture, rather than pouring it all in the middle.

4. Add a few drops of your favorite scented oil. Lavender and vanilla work well.

5. Mix everything together with your hands, breaking up any big lumps you find.

6. Use the mist feature on the spray bottle to add a few squirts of witch hazel into the mixture.

Lemon and strawberry scented oils are nice, too

7. Mix everything together until it feels like damp sand. If it feels too dry, add a little more witch hazel.

8. Press the mixture into the plastic molds. Decorate your *bath bombs* with sprinkles or cake decorations.

9. Squeeze the molds shut and let your *bath bombs* harden for five hours. Is it bathtime yet?

21

Treat yourself

Chocolate truffles

45 mins

Ingredients

- 2 tbsp heavy cream
- ½ tsp vanilla extract
- 1 tbsp butter
- 3½oz (100g) chocolate
- Cocoa powder or coconut shavings

Makes 10

If you know someone with a sweet tooth, there's no better gift than these delicious truffles. They're so easy to make that the hardest part will be not eating them all yourself!

1. Mix the heavy cream, vanilla, and butter in a pan until melted. Break the chocolate into chunks. Stir it into the mixture until melted.

2. Transfer the mixture to a bowl and let it cool. Put it in the freezer for 30 minutes until it thickens, taking it out every 5 minutes to stir.

3. Wash your hands. Take about a teaspoon of the mixture at a time and roll it into balls. Work quickly so your hands don't melt the truffles!

4. Roll the truffles in cocoa powder or coconut shavings and put each one in a mini baking cup.

22

If you're giving the truffles as a gift, put them on a piece of cardboard, wrap them in plastic, and tie it together with ribbon.

Coconut shavings taste yummy

Button jewelry

Making button jewelry is a cheap and easy way to create your own funky, custom jewelry. Grab some colorful buttons and get started with this hair clip, bracelet, and brooch. What else can you make?

1. Stack buttons together with the smallest one on top. Loop craft wire through the button holes.

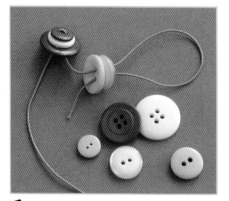

1. Stack a few buttons together and thread elastic string through the holes. Repeat with more buttons.

1. Turn a big button upside down and ask an adult to glue small buttons around the edge using a glue gun.

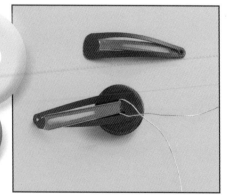

2. Wrap the wire around the top of the hair clip and pull it tight. Tie it in a knot and trim the excess.

2. Repeat until you have a circle, making sure the buttons overlap. Tie the ends of the string together.

2. Let it dry and turn it over. Ask an adult to glue a brooch pin to the back or sew it onto anything you like.

Customize shoes

Plain canvas sneakers are always fashionable, but if you decorate them, not only will they look even cooler, but they'll be totally one of a kind!

You will need
- Canvas sneakers
- All-purpose glue
- Sequins and decorations
- Ribbon
- Clear tape
- Fabric pens

1. Choose a pair of sneakers to decorate. If you're using an old pair, make sure to clean them thoroughly first. Remove the shoelaces.

2. Glue the sequins or decorations to the toes of the sneakers. Make a pattern using different colors.

3. Glue more sequins along the seam under the shoelace eyelets. Leave a gap between each one.

4. Roll up the ends of the ribbon and tape the ends securely so you can lace up your new shoelaces.

Or, try this...

Customize!

It's up to you how you want your sneakers to look. You can use fabric pens to sketch your own design, or get really creative with decorations.

Try either matching or different colored ribbon for the laces

Recycled pom-poms

Making pom-poms takes a bit of patience, but they're a lot of fun and make great decorations. These are made from old plastic bags so are free to make and a great recycling project!

You will need
- Cardboard
- Scissors
- Plastic bags
- String

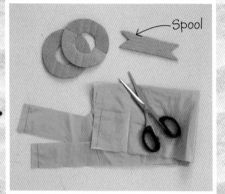
Spool

1. Cut two 3in (7.5cm) circles out of cardboard and cut holes in the middle. Cut a small pice of cardboard to use as a spool, as shown.

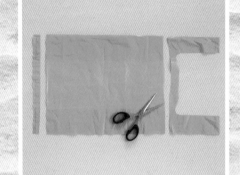

2. Lay one of your plastic bags on its side. Cut off the bottom and the handles and smooth out any wrinkles.

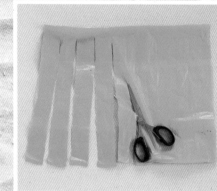

3. From the bottom of the bag, make cuts up to 1in (2.5cm) from the top, leaving 1in (2.5cm) gaps between the cuts.

4. Do the same from the top, making the cuts in between the strips you made already. As before, leave a 1in (2.5cm) gap at the bottom.

5. Cut along the bottom and top of the bag, leaving the top right corner untouched. You'll be left with one long strip to wrap around the spool.

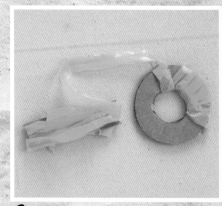

6. Put the two rings together and wrap the plastic around them until you run out. Use the spool to help thread the plastic through the hole.

Flip flops

You can use your pom-poms to decorate clothes, shoes, or bags. Dancers and cheerleaders can use them to shake in their routines. What will you do with yours?

7. Cut the plastic all the way around the outside edge of the cardboard rings. Don't cut all the way through to the middle.

8. Wrap string between the rings and pull it tight. Tie a tight Knot. The string should squeeze the plastic into the gap in the ring.

9. Cut or pull off the cardboard rings. Fluff the pom-pom and trim off any excess string.

Grow your own veg

Growing your own fruits and vegetables isn't difficult. With a little patience and tender loving care, you'll have fresh lettuce, carrots, tomatoes, and potatoes to use in your recipes.

Lettuce

Fill small pots with seed compost and use a pencil to make ½in (1cm) trenches. Sprinkle lettuce seeds into the trenches and cover them with soil. Water the seeds regularly and after about 10 weeks you will have lettuce to harvest!

It's very important to wash everything you grow before you eat it

Do you like red or green lettuce?

Carrots

Fill a deep pot with potting soil. Make a ½in (1cm) trench and fill it with carrot seeds. Cover them with soil and water regularly. After about two weeks, small seedlings will grow. If the pot is crowded, pick some out.

Tomatoes

Cut an egg carton in half. Fill it with potting soil and push a few tomato seeds into each egg cup. Water them regularly and after about two weeks transfer any seedlings to their own pots. Put a stake into the soil next to each plant and tie the stem to it as it grows.

Carrots take about 12 weeks to grow

It will be 20 weeks before you can pick your tomatoes

Potatoes

Plant seed potatoes in holes 6in (15cm) deep and 12in (30cm) apart in the ground. Make sure they are in a place that gets a lot of light. Water regularly and after 20 weeks, dig up one of the plants to see if the potatoes are ready.

Herbs and spices

Just a small pinch of spice or a few chopped herbs can add a lot of flavor to your food. There are many different herbs and spices, but the ones shown here are some of the most useful.

Cinnamon

Vanilla

Paprika

Chives

Mint

Lemongrass

Basil

Dill

Thyme

Ginger

Black pepper

Parsley

Cilantro

Ginger

A common ingredient in South Asian cooking, ginger goes well with vegetables and chicken. It is also tasty in cookies and cakes!

Cinnamon

Popular at Christmastime (and all year round!), cinnamon is used to flavor sweet and savory foods.

Vanilla

Ice creams and desserts are often vanilla-flavored. Vanilla gives sweet foods a lovely flavor and smell.

Paprika

Fiery red in color, paprika adds a hot, spicy zing to foods.

Black pepper

Used to season savory dishes, every table has salt and pepper!

Thyme

Thyme is fairly strong, so add only a little to stews and barbecues.

Mint

Used frequently in Greek cooking, mint goes well with yogurt and lamb. It also makes delicious tea!

Lemongrass

This strongly flavored herb is found in many Thai dishes.

Dill

Delicate dill has a mild, grassy taste and pairs nicely with fish.

Basil

Basil is delicious with fresh tomatoes and in salads.

Chives

Snip chive stems over eggs and add the flowers to salads.

Chilantro

Strong and tangy, cilantro is used in Mexican and Asian cooking.

Parsley

Versatile parsley is a well-known garnish and adds a nice flavor to lots of different foods, including fish and eggs.

33

Strawberry boots

Did you know that you can grow delicious strawberries in your backyard? Planting them in a pot is fine, but where's the fun in that? A pair of old rain boots works just as well and looks so much prettier.

You will need

- Rain boots
- Gravel
- Six strawberry plants
- Soil • Eggshells
- Petroleum jelly

1. Ask an adult to cut a hole on each side of the boots (one higher than the other). Each hole should be about the size of the plant's root ball.

2. Put a little gravel in the bottom of each boot to allow for drainage. Add soil until it's level with the first hole in the side.

3. Push a plant sideways into the first hole, then fill the boot with more soil. When you reach the second hole, put in the second plant.

4. Place a third plant into the top of the boot. Level the soil and press down firmly. Repeat the process with the other boot. Water both boots well.

5. Cover the surface of the boots with broken eggshells to keep slugs away. Feed the plants with tomato food every week.

6. Cover the sides of the boots in petroleum jelly so slugs and snails can't crawl up the sides. Make sure to water your plants regularly.

Your plants will
produce fruit in
about 12 weeks

When the sunflowers have opened, use a pencil to pick out the middle to make a smiley face

Sunflower people

It will take a while, but if you're looking for something fun to do in the summer, you can always grow sunflower people. They'll bring happy faces to any garden!

1. Decorate the paint cans and line them with the bags. Put a layer of gravel in the bottom; fill them with soil, and water generously.

2. Make two holes ½in (1cm) deep in each pot and sow a seed into each one. Cover the seeds with soil, then cover each can with a bag.

3. Put the cans in a sunny place and water the plants sparingly, but often. When leaves appear, take off the bag and discard the smaller plant.

4. It will take about 10 weeks for the flowers to grow. Keep watering the plants and remove any extra sunflower heads that may appear.

37

Healthy eating

Your body needs a lot of different things from a variety of foods to stay healthy. You need foods from all the groups shown here every day.

Protein

Foods such as meat, fish, nuts, eggs, and legumes help your body make new cells and repair tissue. An egg for breakfast and fish for dinner would meet your daily protein needs.

Fats and sugar

Fats such as olive oil, butter, and cheese help with digestion and contain important fatty acids that your body needs. Sugar is a source of energy and is found in cakes, cereals, and chocolate.

Dairy products

Cheese, butter, and milk contain protein, vitamins, and minerals, which are very good for you, particularly for your growing bones. They are high in fat, so you only need a small amount.

Fruits and vegetables

You should try to eat lots of fruits and vegetables. They taste fantastic and are full of the vitamins and minerals that your body needs. Which fruits and veggies are your favorites?

Starchy foods

Pasta, rice, and potatoes are full of carbohydrates, which are a good source of energy. They're also full of vitamins, minerals, and fiber. They should make up about one-third of your diet.

Carbohydrates

These are your main source of energy. You find them in bread, pasta, rice, potatoes, and fruit.

Protein

Used by your body to grow new cells and repair itself, protein is found in meat, poultry, fish, legumes, and dairy products.

Fats

A good source of energy while you are growing, fat is found in dairy products, red meats, cakes, cookies, and fish.

Fiber

Found in cereals, bread, vegetables, and fruit, fiber helps your body digest food.

Minerals

Different minerals have different uses. Calcium is important for healthy bones, and iron is good for your blood. They're found in lots of foods, but are especially common in fruits and vegetables.

Vitamins

Vitamins help to keep your body healthy, especially your teeth and skin. They're mostly found in dairy products, fruits, and vegetables.

Sleepover Games

Hosting a sleepover, but stuck for things to do? There are so many great games you can play—take your pick!

Makeover madness

Place lots of makeup in the center of a circle. On the count of three, each person grabs what she can. Next, everyone chooses a partner. One partner is blindfolded and tries to apply makeup to the other partner. Now swap!

Spin the polish

Ask everyone to bring a favorite nail polish and place all the nail polish in a basket. Roll a die—this will be the number of nails painted. Select a polish and spin the bottle. Who is chosen? Paint the correct number of nails in this color.

Dance idols

Split everyone into small teams and make up dances to your favorite music. Draw score cards on paper and get the other teams to watch and judge. Will you have the X-factor?

Two truths and a lie

Everyone has to think up two truths and one lie about themselves. Take turns presenting all three to the other partygoers and see if anyone can discover which "fact" is the lie—it's harder than you think! Give candy to the winner, or treat her to a deluxe manicure.

Movie trivia

Before the sleepover, pick a movie to watch and write down trivia questions about it. Once your friends arrive, watch the movie. When it's finished, have a contest to see who can answer the most questions correctly.

Grab that spoon!

Put as many spoons as players, minus one, on a table and deal the cards. The dealer discards a card, then the player on her left picks it up and discards one of hers. If you match four cards you take a spoon. Last person to get a spoon loses!

Scary stories

Turn out all the lights and have everyone sit in a circle. Take turns telling your scariest ghost stories. Who's the biggest scaredy cat?

Smoothie sensation

You'll need a blender, plain yogurt, and bowls of different fruits, such as strawberries, blueberries, and bananas. Blend the different fruits with the yogurt. Which smoothie tastes the best?

Use pink and white marshmallows

Hot chocolate

Pour the milk into a saucepan and grate in the chocolate. Mix it together over medium heat for about four minutes, or until the chocolate has dissolved. Add a few drops of flavoring, then pour the hot chocolate into mugs. Add marshmallows, sprinkle cocoa powder over the top, and serve!

Ingredients
- 2 cups milk
- 3½oz (100g) chocolate
- Mint, orange, or vanilla extract
- Marshmallows
- Cocoa powder

Midnight feast

25 mins

One of the best parts of a sleepover is the midnight feast. The next time your friends are over, spoil yourselves rotten with these cookies and hot chocolate.

Ingredients

- 7 tbsp butter, softened
- ½ cup brown sugar, packed
- 1 medium egg, beaten
- ¾ cup all-purpose flour
- 1 tbsp cocoa powder
- 2oz (50g) milk chocolate, chopped
- 2oz (50g) white chocolate, chopped
- ½ tsp baking powder
- ½ cup mini marshmallows

Makes 14

1. Preheat the oven to 375°F (180°C). Line baking sheets with parchment paper. Cream the butter and sugar together in a mixing bowl.

2. Beat the egg into the mixture, and stir in the flour, cocoa powder, half of both types of chocolate, and the baking powder.

3. Place teaspoon-sized spoonfuls of the dough onto the baking sheets. Leave a space between each. Flatten with the spoon. Bake for 5 minutes.

4. Remove the cookies. Press the rest of the chocolate and the marshmallows on top. Bake for 10 minutes, until crisp around the edges.

Banana pancakes

The perfect finish to any great sleepover is a hearty breakfast in the morning. These banana pancakes are great because they not only taste delicious, but they're also really fun to flip!

Ingredients

- 2 tbsp granulated sugar
- ¾ cup all-purpose flour
- ¼ cup whole wheat flour
- 2 tsp baking powder
- ¼ tsp salt • ¾ cup milk
- 1 egg • 2 ripe bananas
- Butter, for frying

Makes 12

1. Sift the sugar, flours, and baking powder into a bowl. Add the salt. Mix together. Make a well in the center.

2. Pour the milk into a liquid measuring cup and crack the egg into it. Whisk with a fork until well mixed.

3. Pour the egg and milk into the well you made in the flour. Stir the mixture with a spoon until creamy.

4. Let the mixture stand for about 30 minutes. Mash the bananas, then stir them into the pancake batter.

5. Heat a pat of butter in a pan. Add three small ladlefuls of batter, each about 3in (7.5cm) across.

6. Cook the pancakes for two minutes. Flip them over and cook for another two minutes.

Flipping crêpes

Pancakes are easy to flip because they're thick. But thin French crêpes are trickier. The secret is to tilt the mixture so it covers the bottom of the pan. After a minute, lift the edges with a spatula to loosen them, then flip the crêpe in the air. Ask an adult to show you how—the last thing you want is crêpes on the ceiling!

Cover your pancakes in yummy maple syrup!

Blueberries and raspberries are delicious with pancakes

Friendship bracelets

Giving someone a friendship bracelet is a great way to show them that they're important to you. It's a bonus that the bracelets are fashionable and easy to make!

Easy

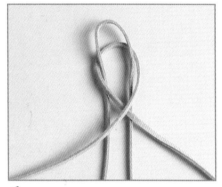

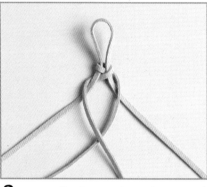

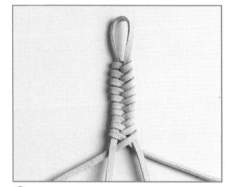

1. Take two pieces of twine about the length of your arm. Make a loop in one and lay it flat, then wrap the second piece around it, as shown.

2. Cross the two ends of the second strand over one another. Wrap them around the outside of the first strand and pull tight to make a knot.

3. Repeat—crossing the ends over one another and going around the first strand—until your bracelet is the desired length. Trim the ends.

Hard

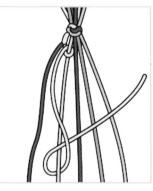

1. Line up six lengths of different colored embroidery floss, each about as long as your arm. Knot them together near the top.

2. Take the first color and loop it over then under the second strand and pull it tight. Repeat this to create a double knot.

3. Do this again over the next color, and then the next, until the first piece has moved all the way to the right side.

4. Repeat this process with the second strand. Continue until the bracelet is long enough. Knot the strands together and trim the ends.

To add decoration, thread beads into your bracelets

World food

Every country has its own signature food, which is almost always a favorite of the kids who live there. How many of these foods have you tried?

Samosas

These spicy, savory treats from India are pastries filled with potatoes and vegetables. They can also be stuffed with ground chicken or lamb.

Samosas are usually served with a tasty chutney

Falafel

Spicy and delicious, falafel is a chickpea pattie popular in the Middle East. It is full of herbs and spices such as cilantro and cumin and is packed with flavor.

Burritos

A traditional Mexican dish, burritos are wrapped wheat tortillas filled with beans, rice, and meats such as beef, pork, and chicken.

Sushi

A Japanese rice dish, sushi is a mixture of rice, raw fish, egg, and vegetables, all wrapped up in a pretty seaweed casing.

Falafel is often served with salad in a warm pita bread

Burritos taste best when they're filled with spicy salsa!

Sushi looks great because you can see all the ingredients inside

Spring rolls

Found all over Southeast Asia, spring rolls are delicious pastry appetizers filled with vegetables, seafood, and meat.

Spring rolls can be crispy or chewy and are often served with a dipping sauce

Strudel

A yummy, fruit-filled pastry dessert from Austria, strudel is served warm, with heavy cream or ice cream.

Most strudels are filled with apple, raisins, and cinnamon

Bruschetta

You will need

- 4 tomatoes
- 6 basil leaves
- 1 tbsp olive oil • Salt and pepper
- Ciabatta, or another Italian bread, sliced
- 1 clove garlic, peeled

1. Halve and seed the tomatoes. Press the seeds through a strainer to extract the juice. Dice the tomato flesh and add it to the juice.

2. Chop the basil and add to the tomatoes. Add the olive oil and season with salt and pepper. Leave the bowl in the fridge for 30 minutes.

3. Toast the bread on both sides. Rub each slice with a clove of garlic, then heap a spoonful of the tomato mixture onto each piece and serve.

Bruschetta is a tasty Italian dish eaten as a snack or an appetizer

49

World customs

It's not just food that's different around the world. Every country has its own customs, traditions, and celebrations, and they might be very different from the ones you know!

Sharing

In some countries people eat from a single large dish placed in the middle of everyone, instead of off separate plates. It's impolite to reach over others and grab the tastiest bites!

Etiquette

If you're eating in Hong Kong you might not want to finish your entire meal, or the host will think he hasn't provided enough food!

In most countries burping is considered very rude, but in China it can be a way of showing that you have enjoyed your meal.

In many countries it's common to eat your meals using only your fingers—but you should only use your right hand to eat.

Choose carefully when buying flowers in Russia—a yellow bouquet can mean that you no longer want to be friends with someone.

Austrians consider it very impolite to be late, but in Mexico it's not a problem to show up a short while after you're expected.

If you're visiting other countries be careful where you point. Pointing can be considered bad manners and a sign of anger.

Festivals

Food is usually a big part of celebrations and festivals—no matter where you are. Here are a few festivals and the foods that help mark them.

Thanksgiving

To celebrate the first harvest of the settlers in North America centuries ago, families get together to eat a feast of roast turkey and pumpkin pie.

Eid ul-Fitr

Eid ul-Fitr is a three-day Islamic festival that follows Ramadan, a holy month when people don't eat or drink during the day. During Eid ul-Fitr, families and friends feast on a variety of sweet treats.

Passover

Passover is the Jewish celebration that remembers when Moses led the Israelites out of slavery in Egypt. Families eat a special meal called Seder, where every type of food has a special meaning.

Using chopsticks

In China, Japan, Korea, and Vietnam most food is eaten with chopsticks instead of with a knife and fork. See if you can do it, too!

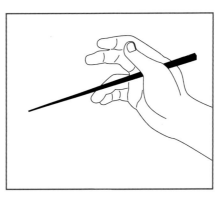

1. Hold one of the chopsticks so that it rests between the crook of your thumb and the top part of your ring finger.

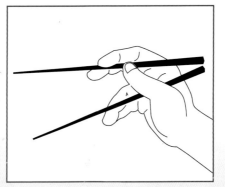

2. Hold the second chopstick between your thumb and index finger. Practice lifting the top chopstick, while keeping the bottom one still.

Keep trying! Practice makes perfect

Trace your family tree

You can learn a lot about yourself by charting your family history. Not only is making a family tree fun, but it will also give you a clearer picture of where you come from.

1. Start by writing your name at the bottom of a large piece of paper. You will probably have to do a few versions of your family tree, so don't worry about making it neat from the start.

2. If you have brothers and sisters, draw a horizontal line above your name and write their names under it, with the oldest on the left and youngest on the right.

If you want to be thorough, you can also add everyone's date of birth!

3. Draw another line upward from the middle of the line. At the top, draw a short horizontal line and write the names of your parents next to it, with your dad on the left, and your mom on the right.

4. If your parents have brothers and sisters, draw a horizontal line above your parents' names and write the names of your aunts and uncles underneath, just as you did for your own brothers and sisters.

5. Draw lines down from your aunts' and uncles' names and write the names of any cousins you have there. Remember to put the oldest person on the left and the youngest on the right.

6. Repeat this process with your grandparents, great-grandparents, and any other family members you have until you have filled in your tree as much as possible.

If your tree is looking messy and you're having trouble fitting everything in, start over until you are happy with it.

Ask your parents if they can help you fill out more. After all, it's their family tree, too!

Make a few different patterns by swirling and whirling the paint colors!

Marbled paper

Marbled paper is great for decorating all kinds of things. Wrap gifts in it, turn it into a stylish background for art projects, or use it as stationery. So many uses—and it's inexpensive and simple to make!

1. In a cup, mix a dollop of paint with four caps of turpentine. Fill the pan with 1in (2.5cm) of water and add a few spoonfuls of paint mixture.

2. Add a second color of paint to the mixture and swish and swirl it around with a toothpick to create an interesting pattern.

3. Lay a sheet of paper on the surface of the water to absorb some of the paint.

4. Pick the paper up by the corners and lift it out of the pan. Lay it on newspaper to dry.

55

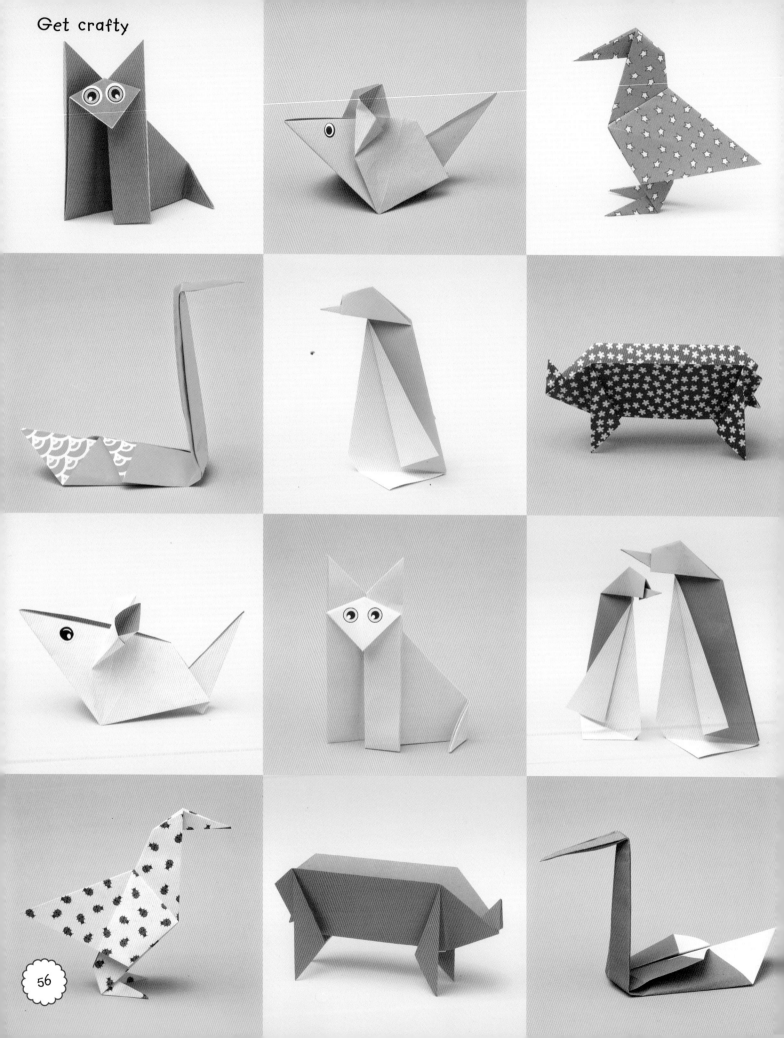

Origami animals

Origami is the traditional Japanese art of folding square paper to create creatures or sculptures. See if you can make these animals just by folding the paper as shown—no cutting or gluing allowed!

You will need
- Square origami paper
- Sticker eyes (optional)

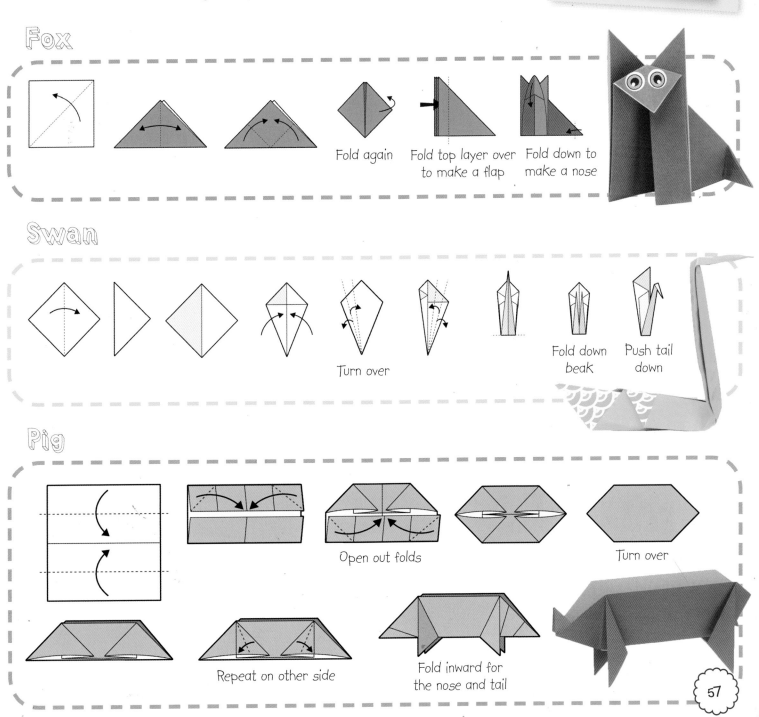

Fox

Fold again

Fold top layer over to make a flap

Fold down to make a nose

Swan

Turn over

Fold down beak

Push tail down

Pig

Open out folds

Turn over

Repeat on other side

Fold inward for the nose and tail

More origami

Once you've mastered the fox, the swan, and the pig, try this mouse and penguin. Remember—practice makes perfect!

Mouse

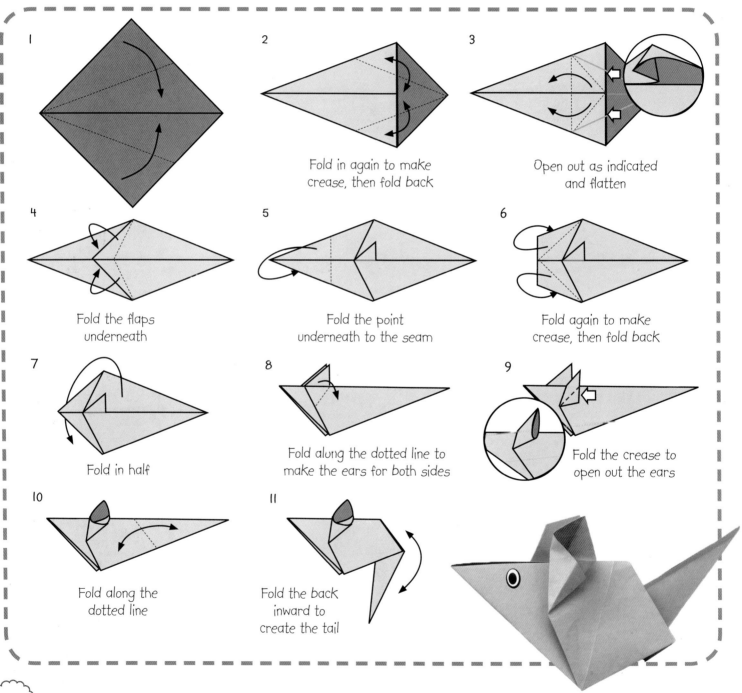

1

2
Fold in again to make crease, then fold back

3
Open out as indicated and flatten

4
Fold the flaps underneath

5
Fold the point underneath to the seam

6
Fold again to make crease, then fold back

7
Fold in half

8
Fold along the dotted line to make the ears for both sides

9
Fold the crease to open out the ears

10
Fold along the dotted line

11
Fold the back inward to create the tail

Penguin

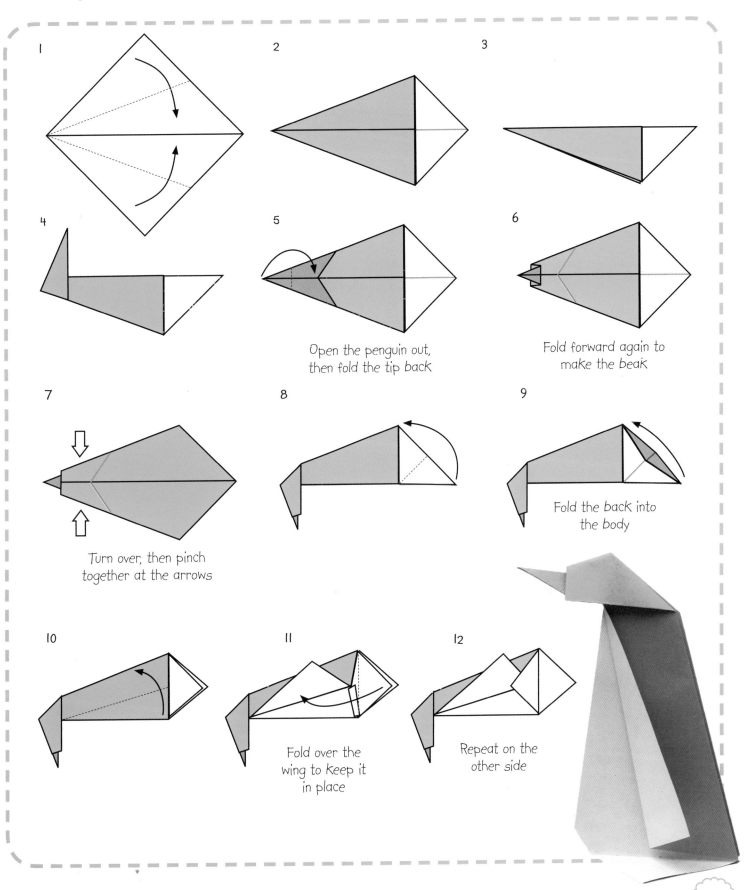

1

2

3

4

5

Open the penguin out,
then fold the tip back

6

Fold forward again to
make the beak

7

Turn over, then pinch
together at the arrows

8

9

Fold the back into
the body

10

11

Fold over the
wing to keep it
in place

12

Repeat on the
other side

Piñata party

Piñatas are a tradition at birthdays and festivals in Mexico. They're stuffed with candy and toys and hung from trees. Children take turns bashing them open to get to the goodies! The next time you're celebrating something, why not make this fluffy owl piñata?

1. Inflate and tie the balloon. Glue strips of newspaper to the balloon, leaving a gap at the bottom where the knot is.

2. Let it dry, and then repeat with two more layers. Pop the balloon with a pin and trim away the knot so you are left with a shell.

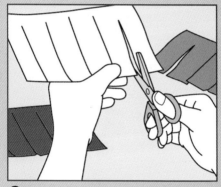

3. Cut the tissue paper into strips and make cuts along the edge to create fringe. Glue layers of paper to the shell, starting from the bottom.

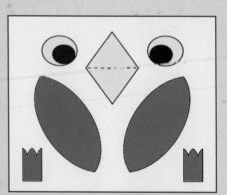

4. Cut out eyes, a beak, feet, and wings from the cardboard and glue them to the shell. Use more tissue paper to decorate the rest of the owl.

5. Make two holes in the top of the piñata with a pencil. Loop a length of string through one hole and out the other. Tie it together.

6. Fill the owl with candy and toys. Cut a piece of cardboard big enough to cover the hole, and use tape to keep it in place.

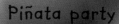

Piñata time!

Whack it!

Hang the piñata from a tree. Players put on a blindfold (a scarf is fine) and take turns swinging at the piñata with a stick. When the treats spill out, it's a free-for-all! Grab some before they're all gone!

This will make a wonderful birthday present for a friend!

Customize your diary

You will need
- Diary
- Colored felt
- Needle and thread
- Buttons • Glue
- Colored elastic
- Mini clothespin
- Wooden toggle

Writing in a diary is a great way of keeping a record of the things you've done, and it's really fun to read what you've written each year. If your diary looks plain and dull, you can customize it with this cute bird design.

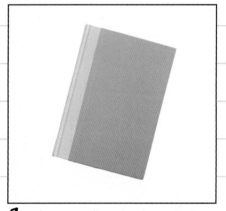

1. Choose a diary to decorate. You can use a brand new one, or if you already have one you can use that.

2. Cut out the shape of a bird from felt. Cut out a smaller version for a wing. Sew a border around the bird, and then sew on the wing.

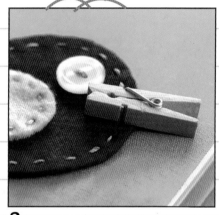

3. Sew on a button for an eye, and glue your bird to your diary. Make legs from elastic and glue them under the bird. A mini clothespin makes a beak.

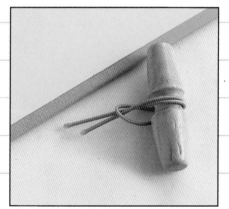

4. Make a loop in a piece of elastic and wrap it around the toggle. Thread the ends back through the loop, and secure the loop in place.

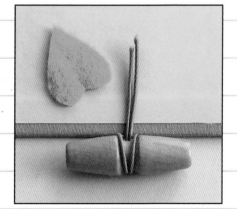

5. Open the diary and position the toggle so that the elastic sits inside the front cover, as shown. Cut out a piece of felt big enough to cover it.

6. Glue the elastic and felt to the inside of the front cover. Once it has dried, decorate your diary with beads, buttons, and sequins.

If you're painting your creatures, it's easier to do it before you glue

Pebble creatures

You can make cool creatures out of almost anything—even pebbles! The next time you're at the beach or in the park look for pebbles in a variety of colors, patterns, and sizes.

1. Gather the things you will need and decide which animals you're going to make. Wash the pebbles well to get rid of any dirt.

2. Glue pebbles in a line to make a caterpillar. It's easy to make and you will become used to gluing pebbles together.

3. For a mouse, add googly eyes. To make ears, cut out pieces of felt, pinch the ends together, and glue them in place.

4. Once you have finished one animal, try making other creatures. Look at your stones carefully. Which animals do they resemble?

65

Pebble flowers

Cute animals aren't the only things you can make from pebbles. You can use them to hold up pretty flowers or even turn them into bases for funky photo frames.

1. Gather all your materials together. If you like, you can paint your pebbles different colors before you start.

2. Thread craft wire through the holes in the button and twist it so that it stays in place.

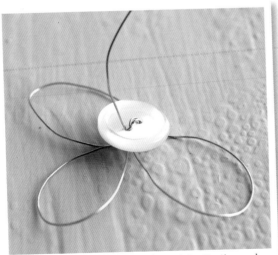

3. Thread the wire back and forth through the holes, bending it each time to make the petal shapes.

4. Wrap the other end of the wire around a large, flat pebble to form the base. Wrap it a few times so it holds firmly. Cut off any excess.

Glue clothespins to the wire to make photo holders

Get crafty

Choose your favorite
colors to decorate
your frame

Make sure you can still see the picture!

68

Customize your frames

It's great to display pictures of your friends, family, vacations, and pets, but some picture frames can look a bit dull. Here are some ways you can jazz them up.

You will need
- Photo frames
- Acrylic paints
- Mini pom-poms, fur trim, beads, glitter, felt, and stickers
- Glue or a glue gun

1. If you have colored frames, skip to step 2. Otherwise, get some plain frames and remove the backing and glass. Paint the frames with different colored acrylic paints (you might need two coats). Once the frames are dry, put the back and glass in again.

2. Squeeze glue on the frame or ask an adult to put dots of glue on the frame with a glue gun. Stick on the pom-poms.

3. Decide how you want to decorate your frames. Experiment with materials such as fur trim, beads, glitter, felt, and stickers.

Making ice cream

There's nothing better than ice cream on a hot summer day. And the best ice cream is homemade. Here's how to make your own.

Ingredients

- Grated zest and juice of 1 lemon
- 2 cups blueberries
- 2 tbsp granulated sugar
- 1¼ cups heavy cream
- 2 cups plain yogurt
- 2 tbsp confectioners' sugar

Serves 4

1. Put the lemon zest and juice, blueberries, and granulated sugar in a pan. Bring the mix to a boil. Simmer 5 minutes, or until the berries burst.

2. Take the pan off the heat. Push the mixture through a strainer into a bowl so that you're left with a smooth purple sauce. Discard the berries.

3. While the sauce cools, beat the cream in a large mixing bowl until it starts to form soft peaks.

4. Add the yogurt and confectioners' sugar and mix together until smooth. Stir in the cooled blueberry sauce.

5. Pour the mixture into a freezer-proof container and freeze for 5 hours. Use a fork to break up ice every hour.

Fast-freeze ice cream

If you're in a hurry and just can't wait, you can use some smart science to make ice cream in just 10 minutes.

Pour ½ cup milk, 1 tbsp granulated sugar, and ½ tbsp pure vanilla extract into a small resealable plastic bag and squeeze out any air. Pour some crushed ice and 2 tbsp of salt into a second, larger resealable plastic bag. Place the small bag into the large one, put on some gloves, and squeeze the bags together. Within a few minutes the ice and salt will have frozen the mixture into delicious ice cream!

Serve your ice cream between two wafers or with some fruit

Ice pops

Looking for fun and fancy ways to cool down during the summer heat? With these fab pops and icy bowl you'll be chilling out in no time.

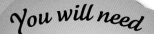
Serves 4

1. Peel the peaches and remove the pits. Chop the peaches into chunks.

2. Put the peaches, orange juice, and sugar into a blender and mix everything until smooth.

3. Pour the mixture into the molds. Add a few pieces of canned fruit salad for a delicious surprise!

4. Push the ice pop sticks into the molds and place the molds in the freezer for about 5 hours

Fruit salad chunks make the ice pops even tastier!

Ice bowl!

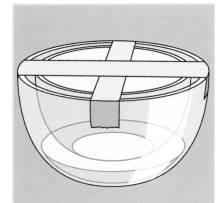

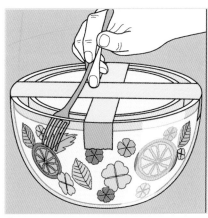

1. Fill a bowl with about 1in (2.5cm) of water and put it in the freezer. Once it's solid, put a smaller bowl on top of the ice, and tape it in place.

2. Pour water into the gap between the two bowls. Add decorations such as fruit slices and leaves and use a fork to spread them around.

3. Put the bowls in the freezer for 10 hours. Remove the tape and turn the bowl upside down so that your ice bowl slides out, ready to use!

Fill your bowl with fresh fruit or ice cream

Your ice bowl will last a few hours

Picnic brownies

If you're going on a picnic, you'll need something sweet to have after your sandwiches. Make these brownies and lemonade ahead of time and pack them in your picnic basket for an afternoon treat.

Makes 12

Ingredients

- 3oz (85g) dark chocolate
- 11 tbsp unsalted butter • ½ tsp salt
- 1 cup all-purpose flour • ½ tsp baking powder • 3 tbsp cocoa powder
- 2 eggs • 2 cups brown sugar
- 1 tsp pure vanilla extract
- 1 cup chopped pecans

1. Preheat the oven to 350°F (180°C). Put the chocolate and butter in a pan over low heat. Stir until melted.

2. Pour the mixture into a bowl. Sift in the salt, flour, baking powder, and cocoa powder, and mix together.

3. In another bowl, mix the eggs, sugar, and vanilla extract. Stir in the chocolate mixture and pecans.

4. Line a baking pan with parchment paper. Pour the mixture into the pan and smooth it out. Bake for 25 minutes. Let cool, then cut into squares.

A cold glass of pink lemonade is the perfect refreshment on a hot summer day, and it goes beautifully with rich brownie treats!

1. Peel the zest from the lemons with a potato peeler and squeeze the juice into a liquid measuring cup.

2. Add the lemon zest and sugar, then pour in the boiling water. Stir it together until the sugar has dissolved.

3. Let the mixture cool, then strain the lemonade into a serving pitcher. Add the cranberry juice, cold water, and ice. Garnish with lemon slices.

Ingredients

- 4 lemons
- ½ cup granulated sugar
- 2¼ cups boiling water
- ¾ cup cranberry juice
- ¾ cup cold water
- Ice
- Lemon slices

75

Summer salads

Here are four tasty salads that are great as snacks or in a picnic basket. Perfect for sharing—all your guests can try a little of each one!

Chicken pasta salad

Serves 4

Ingredients

- 3½oz (100g) dried pasta bows
- 12oz (350g) cooked chicken breast, cubed
- 2 scallions, finely chopped
- ½ tomato, diced
- Juice of ½ lemon
- 3 tbsp yogurt
- 2 tbsp corn
- 3 tbsp mayonnaise
- 2 tbsp chopped dill

Cook the pasta in a saucepan of boiling water for 10 minutes, then drain and rinse it under cold water. Place the cooked pasta in a large bowl and mix in the rest of the ingredients. Keep refrigerated until ready to serve.

Serve the pasta in colorful cups

For a vegetarian version, leave out the chicken and add extra vegetables, such as green beans

Potato salad

Ingredients

- 1lb 2oz (500g) baby new potatoes
- 3 tbsp crème fraîche
- 3 tbsp yogurt

Wash the potatoes and cut them in half. Boil them in a saucepan for 12-15 minutes. While they cool, mix the crème fraîche and yogurt in a bowl. Add this to the potatoes and stir everything together. Keep refrigerated until ready to serve.

Serves 4

Sprinkle chives on top to decorate

Picnic salad

Ingredients

- ½ cucumber, cut into chunks
- ½ red onion, sliced
- 12 cherry tomatoes, cut into quarters
- 2 whole wheat pita breads
- 1 tbsp olive oil
- 5½oz (150g) feta cheese

Put the cucumber, onion, and tomatoes into a large bowl. Toast the pita bread and cut into small pieces. Add the pieces to the salad. Sprinkle olive oil over the top. Toss the salad together. Scatter the feta on top and refrigerate until ready.

Serves 4

Green salad

Ingredients

- 3½oz (100g) green beans
- 3½oz (100g) broccoli
- ¾ cup fresh peas
- 5½oz (150g) salad greens (arugula, baby spinach, etc.)

Dress with your favorite salad dressing

Steam the green beans for two minutes, then add the broccoli and peas and steam for three more. Put the vegetables on top of the salad greens on a large plate, ready to serve.

Serves 4

Make a kite

Whether you're at the beach or in the park, flying a kite is a great way to have summertime fun. Using items you have at home, you can make a one-of-a kind kite that will be prettier than all the rest!

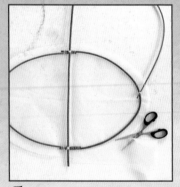

1. Soak the stakes overnight to make them flexible. Wrap thread around two stakes 2in (5cm) from the ends, as shown.

2. Bend one of the stakes toward the middle and secure it in place with the thread. Tie the thread very tightly.

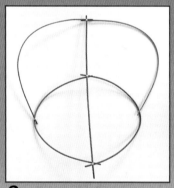

3. Finish the frame by attaching a stake to the other side. Add two more that link them to the top, as shown.

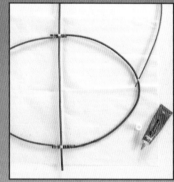

4. Put glue onto the bottom half of your frame. Lay the frame onto tissue paper, with the glue side down.

5. Once the glue has dried, cut around the shape of the frame, leaving a border of about 2in (5cm).

6. Cut the border into small strips and then fold them over the stake and glue them in place.

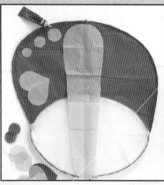

7. Repeat this with another piece of tissue paper. Where the two pieces meet, trim the paper and glue to the stake.

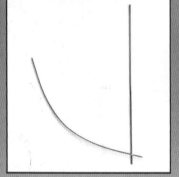

8. Turn the kite over. Cut out a strip of tissue paper for the body and glue it in place. Add other pieces to decorate.

Wait for a breezy day and then go out and fly your kite!

9. Cut and fold five long strips of tissue paper to make streamers. Line up the ends and staple together.

10. Glue the streamers to the bottom of the kite. Cut two lengths of kite string 2in (5cm) longer than your kite.

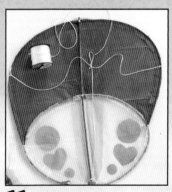

11. Tie one length around the stake at the bottom and the other to each side, making a small hole in the tissue paper.

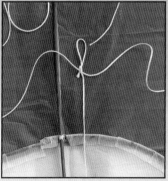

12. Tie the bottom string to the horizontal string and make a loop. Thread the rest of the kite string through the loop.

Balloon animals

Animal balloons are a hit at any party—and they're a lot easier to make than it appears! Start by making the swan first, then move on to the poodle. Get your friends in on the act, too. Whose animal do you think will look the best?

You will need

- Modeling balloons

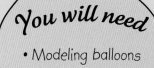

Swan

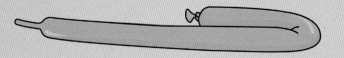

1. Inflate a balloon, leaving about 4in (10cm) deflated, and tie a knot. Make a fold about 8in (20cm) away from the knot.

2. Fold the tail again so the end lines up with the first fold. The balloon should fold like a paperclip.

3. Where all three parts meet—by the knot—twist everything together. You should have two loops and a tube sticking up, as shown.

4. Pull one of the loops up through the other to make the body. The long tube will be the swan's neck and head.

5. Fold the neck away from the body, as shown. So it keeps this shape, hold it tightly and squeeze out some of the air.

Poodle

1. Inflate a balloon, leaving a 7in 18cm) tail. Make a bubble about 2in (5cm) for the head and another one 2in (5cm) away.

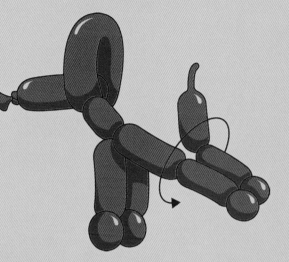

4. Leave a gap about 3in (7.5cm) long for the body, then repeat what you did in step 3 to make the hind legs.

2. Make a fold where the knot meets the twist, creating a loop. Then push the head (the bubble with the knot) through it.

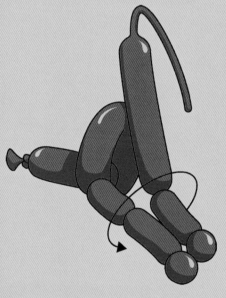

3. Leave a gap, then make a 3in (7.5cm) bubble, two 1in (2.5cm) bubbles, and a 3in (7.5cm) bubble. Twist the last bubble into the first one to make the front legs.

5. Twist everything and straighten it out. Finally, squeeze the tail so that some of the air forms a bubble at the back.

Caramel popcorn

Warm, homemade popcorn is a delicious treat, and it's tastier still when you add a caramel topping. Popcorn is great at any get together, but it's especially good on a movie night. Afterward, serve these chocolately banana bites.

Ingredients

- 2 tbsp corn oil
- ½ cup popcorn kernels
- 4 tbsp butter
- ¼ cup light brown sugar, packed
- 5 tbsp corn syrup

1. Pour the oil into a saucepan and place over medium heat. Add the corn kernels; cover with a lid. Have an adult shake the pan while the kernels pop.

2. In another pan, stir the butter, sugar, and syrup together over medium heat, until everything has blended into a caramel sauce.

3. When the popcorn is ready, put it in a large bowl and coat it evenly with the sauce. Mix all ingredients well with a spoon, let cool, and enjoy!

You know your corn is nearly ready when the pops are a few seconds apart

Banana bites

1. Break the chocolate into pieces and add to a bowl. Place the bowl over a pan of warm water. Stir the chocolate until melted.

2. Chop the bananas into even-sized chunks. Push a straw through the center of each piece and place them on a plate.

3. Spoon the chocolate over the bananas and coat them evenly. Roll them in sprinkles and place in the refrigerator to set.

Makes 15

Why not try chocolate sprinkles?

Coconut shavings are yummy, too

You will need
- 6oz (150g) chocolate
- 2-3 bananas
- Straws
- Sprinkles

Have fun frosting and decorating your cupcakes with sprinkles and candies

84

Cupcake heaven

30 mins

These cupcakes are perfect for a tea party. Once they are baked, get creative and decorate them with frosting and candies. Try not to eat them all at once!

Ingredients
- 11 tbsp butter, softened
- ¾ cup granulated sugar
- ½ cup self-rising flour
- ½ tsp pure vanilla extract
- 3 eggs, whisked

For the frosting
- 2 cups confectioners' sugar
- 2–3 tbsp water
- Food coloring

Makes 20

1. Preheat the oven to 350°F (180°C). Line your muffin pans with baking cups. You'll need enough for 20 cupcakes.

2. Mix the butter and sugar together until creamy. Add the flour, vanilla, and eggs. Stir until all ingredients are well combined.

3. Spoon the mixture into the baking cups and place the pans in the oven. Bake for 15 minutes, or until they are firm and golden.

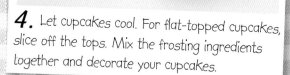

4. Let cupcakes cool. For flat-topped cupcakes, slice off the tops. Mix the frosting ingredients together and decorate your cupcakes.

Baking bread

2½ hours

There's nothing quite like the smell of freshly baked bread—and it's easier to make than you'd think. You can also use this dough in other recipes, and to make rolls and pizza.

Ingredients

- 1½ tsp active dry yeast
- 1 tsp granulated sugar
- 1½ cups warm water
- 3¾ cups white bread flour
- 2 tsp of salt • 1 tbsp olive oil
- 1 egg, beaten

1. Mix the yeast and sugar with half of the warm water. Let it stand in a warm place for about 10 minutes, or until it starts to bubble.

2. Sift the flour and salt into a bowl and make a well in the center. Pour in the yeast mixture, the oil, and the remaining water, and mix well.

3. Put a little flour on your hands and the work surface, and knead the dough for 10 minutes, until it's smooth.

4. Place the dough in a large bowl and cover it with plastic wrap. Put it in a warm (not hot) place for an hour, or until it has doubled in size.

5. Preheat the oven to 425°F (220°C). Push your fist into the dough to punch some of the air out of it. Then knead it for another 5 minutes.

6. Put the dough in a greased loaf pan. Let it stand in a warm place for another 10 minutes to rise. Brush it with the egg, then bake for 30 mins.

Making rolls

Instead of putting the dough in the loaf pan, divide it into small balls. Flatten them slightly and let rise for 30 minutes. Brush with milk and top with seeds, then bake for 25 minutes.

Pizza toppings

The great thing about pizza is that by changing the toppings you can create pizzas with very different flavors. Which one is your favorite?

Ham and pineapple

Ingredients
- 2-3 tbsp tomato purée
- 3 slices ham, cut into strips
- A few pineapple chunks, sliced
- Mozzarella cheese, shredded

1. Make the pizza dough from scratch (*see pages 86-87*). Roll it into disks 7in (18cm) across.

2. Preheat the oven to 425°F (220°C). Spread the tomato purée over the dough. Add the toppings. Bake for 20 minutes, until golden.

Pepperoni and pepper

Ingredients
- 2-3 tbsp tomato purée
- Pepperoni slices
- Half a yellow bell pepper, sliced
- Mozzarella cheese, shredded

Serves 4

Tomato and Olives

Ingredients
- 2-3 tbsp tomato purée
- 3 tomatoes, sliced
- Black olives, sliced
- Fresh basil leaves

Cheese-free pizza is delicious, too!

Mushroom and mozzarella

Ingredients
- 2-3 tbsp tomato purée
- 5oz (125g) mushrooms, sliced
- Mozzarella cheese, shredded

Other toppings
Here are other toppings to choose from. Try several at once.
- Sausage (cooked)
- Chicken (cooked)
- Onions
- Jalapeño peppers
- Bacon (cooked)
- Meatballs (cooked)
- Avocado
- Spinach
- Egg

If you're making recipes that you aren't sure you'll like, divide the pizza into quarters and put different toppings on each section. This way, if you don't like one you haven't ruined the whole pizza!

Dips and nibbles

Here are three great dips to share with friends, all of which can be made in a matter of minutes. Here's how.

Guacamole

Ingredients
- 3 ripe avocados
- ½ red onion, diced
- 1 garlic clove, crushed
- Juice of 1 lime • 2 tomatoes, seeded and diced
- 3 tbsp chopped cilantro

Good guacamole should contain nice big chunks

1. Cut the avocados in half and remove the pits. Scoop out the flesh, chop it up, and put it in a bowl.

2. Add the rest of the ingredients and season with salt and pepper. Mash everything together and serve.

Hummus

Ingredients

- 14oz can chick peas, drained
- ½ tsp ground cumin
- 1 garlic clove, chopped
- 3 tbsp olive oil
- 2 tbsp tahini paste
- Juice of ½ lemon

1. Put all the ingredients into a food processor and blend until smooth. It's that easy!

If you like spice, sprinkle a little paprika on top

Melt a little cheese on the tortillas. Sprinkle with sea salt and freshly ground pepper for perfect dipping chips!

Salsa

Ingredients

- 12oz (350g) tomatoes
- ½ red onion, finely chopped
- Juice of ½ lime
- ¼ cup cilantro, chopped
- 1 jalapeño pepper, chopped
- 2 garlic cloves, chopped

1. Cut the tomatoes in half, remove the seeds, and dice the flesh. Mix with the other ingredients.

For the template

- Two 7 x 4in (18 x 10cm) cardboard rectangles for the roof
- Two 6 x 4in (15 x 10cm) cardboard rectangles for the sides (cut holes for windows)
- Two 4in (10cm) cardboard squares for the ends, extending 3in (7½cm) from the top edge of the squares to a point.

Use the remainder of the icing to attach candy for decoration

Gingerbread house

Making a gingerbread house is a fun way to combine cooking and crafts. It's a bit tricky, but the end result will be impressive—not to mention delicious!

Ingredients

- 18 tbsp unsalted butter, softened
- 1 cup brown sugar
- 2 medium eggs
- ½ cup corn syrup
- 2 tbsp ground ginger

- 2 tsp baking soda
- 4¾ cups all-purpose flour
- 1 egg white
- 1¾ cups confectioners' sugar
- Marshmallows and other candy

1. In a food processor, blend the butter and sugar until creamy. Add the eggs, syrup, ginger, baking soda, and flour. Blend again until smooth.

2. Wrap the dough in plastic wrap and put it in the refrigerator for 30 minutes while you mark and cut out the templates (see opposite).

3. Preheat the oven to 350°F (180°C). Roll the dough out to ¼in (0.5cm) thickness. Cut six pieces using the templates. Lay on a lined baking sheet.

4. Bake the gingerbread for 12 minutes. Let cool. Mix the egg white and confectioners' sugar in a bowl and use it to stick the pieces together.

Gingerbread

If you're in the mood for something a easier than making a gingerbread house, you can always go back to basics and bake delicious gingerbread cookies. Don't forget to decorate them!

Makes 10

You will need

- 4¾ cups all-purpose flour
- 2 tsp baking soda
- 2 tbsp ginger
- 18 tbsp unsalted butter, softened
- 1 cup brown sugar
- 2 eggs
- ⅓ cup molasses

1. Sift the flour, baking soda and ginger into a mixing bowl.

2. Mix the butter and sugar in a second bowl until it's nice and smooth.

3. Add the eggs to the butter mixture and beat together. Add the molasses slowly, stirring to mix well.

4. Add the flour mixture a few spoonfuls at a time, mixing it together as you go.

5. Flatten the dough and wrap it in plastic wrap. Put it in the refrigerator for an hour until it firms up.

6. Preheat the oven to 350°F (180°C). Roll the dough out to a ⅛in (3mm) thickness and cut out shapes with a cookie cutter. Bake for 15 minutes.

Use colored icing when decorating

Decoration

Use different shaped cookie cutters, such as angels, stars, and snowmen. Decorate the cookies with candy and writing icing.

Folded napkins

Make a statement when you set the table with these funky folded napkins. Not only are they quick to make, but you can also use them to hold cutlery, as place settings, or as napkin caddies. They are sure to brighten up any birthday meal!

You will need

- Colored paper napkins
- Glitter and gems
- Craft glue

1. Unfold two different colored napkins and place one on top of the other. Fold them in half twice.

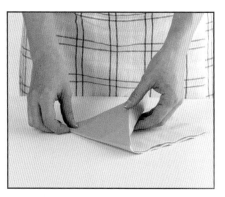

2. Take the top loose corner of the first napkin and fold it underneath to form a pocket.

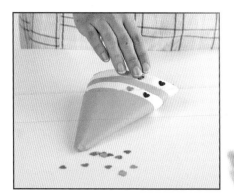

3. Repeat with the other layers, leaving a ½in (1cm) strip between each fold.

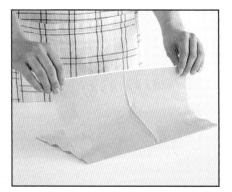

4. Turn the napkins over and fold the two side corners into the center to create a cone shape.

5. Decorate with gems, glitters, and sparkles. Open the pocket to place your cutlery inside.

Color-coordinate these napkins with place settings

Drink stirrers

If you're making fancy party drinks, add these decorative stirrers into the glasses. The drinks look that much nicer, and guests can keep their shakes and drinks well mixed. If you wash the stirrers thoroughly they can be reused!

1. Cut two identical butterfly shapes out of colored cardboard. Bend the wings back and glue them to the top part of the straw.

2. Decorate the butterflies with gems and stickers. Then make more mixers in different shapes, such as stars or flowers.

Create other folded napkins such as these. Or, if you're feeling extra creative, come up with your own styles and designs!

Handmade cards

The next time you want to wish someone a happy birthday, instead of buying them a card make one. You can design the card to look exactly how you like, and, because you made it, it will be extra special!

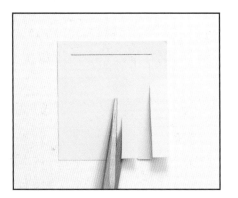

1. Draw a line in pencil on a square piece of paper 1in (2.5cm) from the top. Cut strips every 1in (2.5cm) along the bottom, toward the line.

2. Cut 1in- (2.5cm-) wide strips from a different color of paper. Thread them over and under the strips, making a weave.

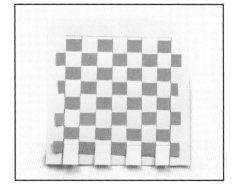

3. Continue weaving until you have a checkerboard pattern. Glue the flaps at the edge to secure them.

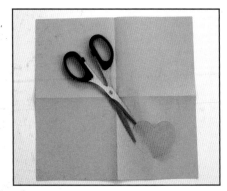

4. Fold a larger piece of paper in half twice and then unfold it so it looks like this. Cut out a shape in the bottom right-hand corner.

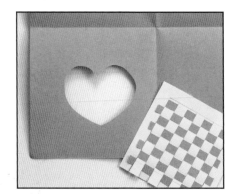

5. Glue your checkerboard pattern to the back side of the solid colored paper so that it shows through the cut-out shape.

6. Fold the paper again to make a square. Now all you need to do is write your message inside.

98

Origami heart

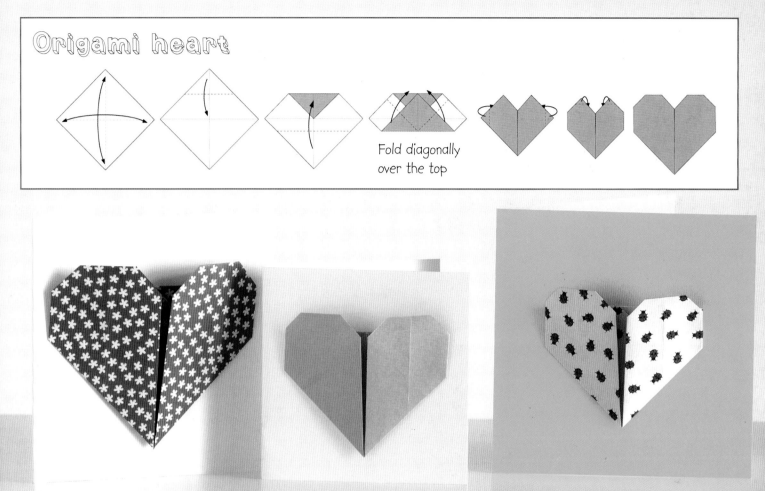

Fold diagonally over the top

Make origami hearts and glue them to give your cards for a cool 3-D effect

Weave in a third colored strip to make this pattern

Glue or draw on other decorations

Party invitations

The next time you're having a party, design and create your own invitations and place settings. They will look great, and everyone will be impressed by your creativity!

You will need

• White and pink card stock paper
• Glue • Colored paper
• Felt shapes, sequins, ribbons, and glitter
• Envelopes

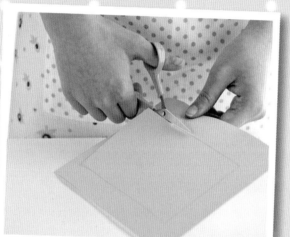

1. Fold the white card stock paper in half. Cut the pink paper to the same size. Draw a 1in (2.5cm) border. Cut it out to make a frame.

2. Stick the frame to the front of the white card. While the glue dries, cut out balloon and present shapes from the colored paper.

3. Decorate the frame with felt shapes, sequins, gems, and ribbon. Glue your paper decorations to the card and add glitter.

4. Wrap ribbon around the envelopes, and glue on more sequins. Don't forget to write in the cards before you seal them!

Party invitations

Place settings

Divide a piece of paper into three equal sections and trim any excess. Fold your card paper into a triangle shape so that one middle section acts as a base. Secure the triangle with tape. Cut out a heart shape from the colored paper and glue it to the front. Decorate with sequins, ribbons, and glitter, then write your friends' names on the front.

You will need

- Colored card stock paper
- Tape • Colored paper
- Glue • Sequins, ribbons, and glitter

Gift boxes

You will need
- Plain boxes
- Paintbrush and paints
- Colored paper or felt
- Glue • Glitter and beads
- Ribbons
- Tissue paper

Fabulous wrapping and packaging really make a difference when you're giving gifts. Fill these beautiful boxes with scrumptious treats and give them to a friend—you're sure to make their day.

Filling
You can fill your boxes with anything you think your friends will like. Candy and chocolates are great, or you can use the boxes for jewelry.

Make each box special and individual

1. Paint the outside of your boxes and let them dry. Cut out flowers and stars from paper or felt, and glue them to the lids.

2. Decorate the boxes with glitter and beads, and wrap ribbon around the outside. Line the inside of each box with tissue paper.

Ribbon, lace, and flowers look great as decorations

Use round, square, or heart-shaped boxes

Birthday cake

No birthday is complete without a great big delicious cake. This recipe will be loved by grown-ups, too!

Ingredients

- 12 tbsp butter, softened
- 1¼ cups brown sugar
- 1¼ cups self-rising flour
- 5 tbsp cocoa powder
- ½ tsp baking soda
- 3 eggs, beaten
- ½ cup sour cream

For the frosting

- 6 tbsp butter
- 6oz (175g) while chocolate
- ¼ cup milk
- 1⅔ cups confectioners' sugar

1. Preheat the oven to 375°F (170°C). Line two 8in (20cm) cake pans with parchment paper.

2. Beat the butter and sugar in a bowl. Add the flour, cocoa powder, baking soda, eggs, and sour cream. Mix together until smooth.

3. Divide the mixture evenly between the cake pans and smooth the tops. Bake the cakes for about 25-30 minutes, until the top feels springy.

4. Turn out the cakes onto a cooling rack. Remove the parchment paper. While they are cooling, make the frosting.

5. Put the butter, chocolate, and milk in a bowl over a pan of simmering water. When the mixture has melted, stir in the confectioners' sugar.

6. Once the frosting has cooled, spread it on one cake layer, then place the other on top. Spread the rest on top and around the sides.

Decoration

Your cake will look and taste even better if you decorate it with candy. For variety, mix different colors and shapes. Don't forget the candles!

Add chocolate shavings and mini balls for a grown-up cake

Try not to eat it all at once!

These bags will make a perfect gift

Put your scented bags in a drawer with your clothes to make them sweet-smelling

Filling

Fill your bags with dried lavender or pot pourri and tie ribbon around the top of each bag to close it up.

Scented bags

If you're cleaning out your closets, don't throw away your old clothes—recycle them! You won't believe how easy it is to turn an old sweater into a pretty scented bag to go in your drawers.

You will need
- 10 x 7in (25 x 18cm) paper template
- Old wool sweater
- Pins • Needle and thread
- Ribbon and buttons
- Dried lavender or pot pourri

1. Cut off a large piece of the sweater and lay it flat. If you want to use the sleeves, cut them off and turn them inside out.

2. Pin the paper template to the fabric and cut around it to make two rectangles. Put the pieces on top of each other and pin together.

3. Sew around the edges of your rectangles, leaving ½in (1cm) around the edge. Leave one edge unsewn, and turn the bag inside out.

4. Cut small hearts or other shapes from any spare fabric and sew them to the front of your bags. Sew on buttons to decorate.

Glove change purses

Turn an old pair of gloves or mittens into a funky change purse or a little bag to hold odds and ends. Make some for your friends, too!

You will need
- Old gloves
- Needle and thread
- Pins
- Zippers
- Buttons and beads
- Scraps of felt, yarn, and ribbon

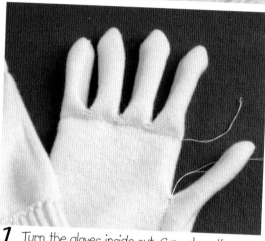

1. Turn the gloves inside out. Sew along the bottom of the fingers and along the thumb. This closes the glove and keeps items from falling out.

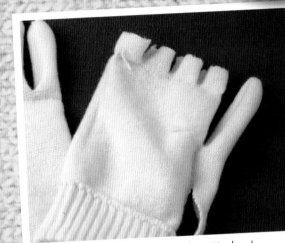

2. Cut the fingers and thumbs off about ¼in (.5cm) from the seam you made. Turn the gloves right side out.

3. Using a zipper that is the same length as the cuff, pin and sew the zipper into the cuff end.

4. Use buttons, beads, felt, yarn, and ribbon to decorate your change purses. Make them look like people or animals.

Theme your bags

If you're planning to make a few little bags, pick a theme and try to make them match. If they're going to be Christmas presents, for example, you could make a snowman, a reindeer, and a Santa change purse.

Felt decorations

You will need
• Colored felt
• Needle and thread
• Beads, buttons, and sequins
• Batting

You can make these to pretty decorations to sew onto a bag or pillow or hang them on their own around your room. Use whatever scraps of felt you have handy.

1. Decide what you're going to make and cut the shapes out from different colors of felt. This design is a pretty cupcake.

2. Use the needle and thread to sew the pieces to a background. Choose a color of thread that shows up on the fabric.

3. Glue or stitch beads, sequins, or buttons to add detail to your design.

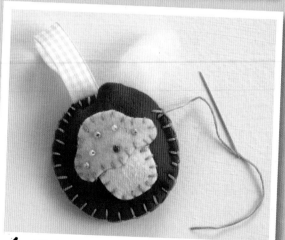

4. Stitch your design to another piece of felt and stuff batting between them. Add a ribbon to make a hanger, and sew the edges to finish.

You can make birds, hearts, and flowers

Attach beads and sequins as decorations

111

Putting up decorations really gets you into the Christmas spirit. For a festive look, make garlands to hang over the fireplace this December.

1. Cut your favorite Christmas designs out of colored felt. You'll need two identical pieces for each one. Pin the felt together.

2. Sew around the edge of your felt then remove the pins. Add details such as eyes using thread, buttons, or colored pens.

3. Add other pieces of felt and buttons as decorations. Thread a piece of wire through the top of each shape and twist it to make a loop.

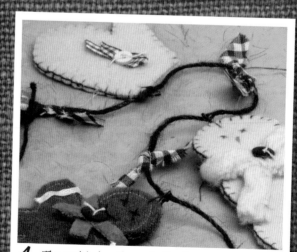

4. Thread twine through the loops to attach your decorations. To finish, tie ribbon to the twine and your garlands are ready to hang.

A pretty garland can be draped about your Christmas tree!

Beaded insects

Hang butterflies and dragonflies from your blinds or curtains, or in your windows, where they can sparkle in the light. They also make pretty necklaces to give as gifts.

1. Unspool about 12in (30cm) of craft wire. Thread a few black beads and then a white one onto the wire to make the body.

2. Take the end of the craft wire back down through the top three beads and then out the side. Leave a small loop at the top.

Bottom wire

3. Push the wire at the bottom back through the beads and out the left side. Thread beads onto the wire on the right to make a wing.

4. Twist the wing so that it stays in place. Repeat this for the bottom wing to complete the first side.

5. Do the same thing on the other side of the butterfly. Try to bend all four wings so they are similar in shape and size.

6. Twist the wires around the body a few times to keep the beads in place. Trim any excess wire with scissors.

Thread ribbon through the loop to make pendants

Flatten the wings a little for dragonfly wings

Car trip games

Going on trips is fun, but the car ride can be boring. Everyone has heard of "I spy," but there are lots of other fun games to help pass the time.

Backseat bingo

Everyone makes a list of things they think they might see along the way, such as landmarks, animals, and signs. When each person sees something on their list they shout it out and cross it off the list. The winner is the first person to see everything on their list.

Car pool

Take turns choosing a color (other than black or white). The goal is to spot seven cars of that color followed by a black one. If another player spots a white car before you finish, it becomes their turn!

City alphabet

Everyone takes turns naming towns or cities. Each town has to begin with the last letter of the one that came before it. So, if the first city is New York, the next could be Kalamazoo. The game continues until someone gets stuck!

Alphabet challenge

Think of a theme, such as going grocery shopping. One player makes a statement ending with a word that starts in "a." Other players takes turns adding things with the next letter. So the person starting says, "I went shopping and bought an apple." The next person could add "banana," and the third "cookies." The goal is to make it all the way to "z."

Music games

Everyone loves getting together with their friends and listening to music. With these musical games, you'll be the hit of any party.

Can you do the moonwalk?

Dance mania

Get everyone to write a random word on a piece of paper, fold each paper, and put them all in a hat. Pass the hat around and everyone chooses a paper (if they choose their own word they have to pick again). Turn on some music and choose someone to start the game. Their job is to come up with a dance based on the word they picked. If the word was "bird" the dance could involve flapping arms and strutting like a rooster. The game continues until everyone has invented a dance. Vote on who created the best dance.

Name that tune

Give everybody a piece of paper and have each person write the numbers 1–10 in a column. Play the first 5 or 10 seconds of a song, then stop the music. Have everyone guess the name of the song and write it on the paper. Do this for 10 songs. Whoever gets the most right answers wins.

Musical statues

Pick someone to be the judge. Their job is to play music while everyone else dances. After a few seconds the judge stops the music. When this happens, everyone freezes in place! If the judge sees anyone move, that person is out! The winner is the last player left.

Musical bingo

Lay out pieces of cardboard on the floor in a big circle. Write a number on each piece—one for every player. Write the same numbers on slips of paper and put them in a bag. Play music and have everyone dance around the circle. Stop the music and tell everyone stand on the piece of cardboard nearest them. Take a piece of paper from the bag and read out the number. Whoever is standing on that number leaves the game and takes their number with them. The last person left wins a prize!

Magic flowers

You will need
- A white flower with a long stem
- 2 glasses or vases
- Tape
- Food coloring

Did you know you can change the color of a flower? Not convinced? Try this experiment and see for yourself: it's like magic!

1. Lay your flower on a cutting board. Ask an adult to cut the stem lengthwise up to about the halfway point.

2. Wrap tape at the point where the cut was made to stop the stem from splitting more.

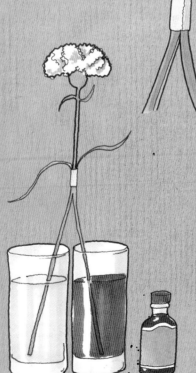

3. Fill the glasses with water. Add food coloring to one of them and mix. Stand the flower in the glasses, with one half of the stem in each glass. In a few hours, half of the petals will have changed color.

Carnations and large daisies work very well for this

Xylem

How this works

Plants draw water from the soil through their roots. Water travels up the stem through a hollow tube called the xylem. In this case, as the water is drawn up from the glass the food coloring travels with it, dying the petals once it reaches the top.

Because the stem is cut in half, the food coloring only travels up half the xylem, which is why all the flower petals don't change color.

Horoscopes

Some people believe that the date of your birth affects your personality, and that you can predict the future by observing the stars. This is called astrology.

There are 12 different star signs. This is because the Sun passes through 12 constellations in a year. Astrologers split these signs into four groups that share similar traits: Earth, fire, air, and water. But each sign has its own unique traits and its own symbol (usually an animal).

Pisces
Feb 19—Mar 20
(The Fish)

Aries
Mar 21—Apr 19
(The Ram)

Aquarius
Jan 20—Feb 18
(The Water Bearer)

Taurus
Apr 20—May 20
(The Bull)

Capricorn
Dec 22—Jan 19
(The Goat)

Gemini
May 21—Jun 20
(The Twins)

Sagittarius
Nov 22—Dec 21
(The Archer)

Cancer
Jun 21—Jul 22
(The Crab)

Scorpio
Oct 23—Nov 21
(The Scorpion)

Leo
Jul 23—Aug 22
(The Lion)

Libra
Sept 23—Oct 22
(The Scales)

Virgo
Aug 23—Sept 22
(The Maiden)

Earth signs

Politeness and sociability are said to be among the traits of those born under Earth signs.

Taurus: Dependable, smart, sporty

Virgo: Creative, intelligent, helpful

Capricorn: Wise, disciplined, calm

Air signs

Being born under an air sign is supposed to make a person curious and good at communicating.

Aquarius: Creative, inventive, friendly

Gemini: Sociable, energetic, childlike

Libra: Kind, artistic, outgoing

Water signs

People born under a water sign are generally sensitive and good at reading people.

Pisces: Dreamy, popular, artistic

Cancer: Gentle, caring, nurturing

Scorpio: Passionate, focused, intense

Are they accurate?

Now that you know the traits of all the star signs, you can put them to the test. Get together with your friends and ask them what their star signs are. Do their personalities match the descriptions?

Fire signs

Anyone born under a fire sign is thought to be bright and strong, but can also be reckless.

Aries: Independent, energetic, intelligent

Leo: Ambitious, active, confident

Sagittarius: Lively, adventurous, optimistic

Chinese horoscopes

Chinese astrology works differently. Again, there are 12 different signs, but each one is based on the year a person was born. So anyone born in 2013 would be born in the "Year of the Snake."

Glossary

Acrylic paint
A fast-drying, water-based paint often used in arts and crafts.

All-purpose glue
A type of glue suitable for use on many different surfaces, such as wood, glass, metal, and textiles.

Baking soda
A chemical in baked goods that makes them rise.

Batting
A layer of material—normally cotton, polyester, or wool—that provides insulation or padding in crafts such as quilting.

Blender
A kitchen appliance with a rotating blade; it can purée and mix foods.

Bulletin board
A corkboard that hold items such as letters, postcards, and photographs. Messages are secured with thumbtacks or push pins, making it easy to add and remove items.

Cork
A material harvested from bark, often used as flooring, in bulletin boards, or as bottle stoppers.

Corn oil
Oil extracted from corn, commonly used for frying.

Craft wire
Metal wire used in crafts. It is flexible and can be made from a variety of metals, such as copper and brass.

Dulce de leche
A sweet, caramel-like substance popular in South America; it is made by slowly heating sweetened milk.

Embroidery floss
A fine thread made specifically for embroidery.

Emulsion paint
A quick-drying, versatile paint frequently used on large areas such as walls and ceilings; it can also be used on wooden furniture.

Fusible webbing
A sticky material used to hem garments, as an alternative to hand-stitching.

Glue gun
An appliance for heating and applying glue at high temperatures; it is ideal for gluing hard materials such as plastic and wood.

Origami paper
Paper specifically designed for origami. It is available in different colors and patterns.

Petroleum jelly
A colorless, translucent ointment frequently used on chapped lips and skin.

Polyethylene bags
A type of plastic bag used for carrying shopping.

Popcorn kernels
The kernels of corn that expand and puff up when heated to make popcorn.

Potting soil
Potting soil consists of decomposed organic material mixed with soil; its rich soil aids in plant growth.

Primer paint
Paint applied to mask imperfections in a painted surface and to protect the top coat from chips.

Sandpaper
A heavy, abrasive paper used to remove material from surfaces, often to make them smoother.

Satin enamel paint
A paint designed for interior wood; it has a slightly glossy surface that can be wiped clean.

Sour cream
A mildly sour, thick cream. It is popular in salad dressings, baking, and South American cuisine.

Staple gun
A sturdy, handheld device that can drive staples into paper, wood, plastic, and masonry. Unlike an office stapler, it does not need to be placed on each side of the material being stapled.

Suede twine
Narrow laces of thin, soft leather.

Tomato purée
Tomatoes mashed or chopped to a fine consistency and a key ingredient in pizza recipes.

Turpentine
A liquid solvent that can thin oil-based paint; it is obtained by distilling tree resin.

Vanilla
A flavoring taken from the vanilla orchid; it is a common ingredient in baked goods and perfumes.

Whisk
A handheld utensil used to blend recipe ingredients.

Witch hazel
A substance extracted from the witch hazel plant; it is helpful in healing skin blemishes and bruising.

Index